Christmas Activities

for KS1 Maths

Irene Yates

Brilliant Publications

Answers

Page 8
The odd star has 6 points and is larger

Page 11
3 Christmas trees; 5 stars; 2 Santas; 6 presents
Extra: 16 things

Page 12
4 mince pies; 9 puddings; 6 candles

Page 13
7 teddies; 5 cars; 3 trains; 4 elephants; 10 toys
Extra: 10

Page 15
6; 7; 8; 9; 10

Page 16
4; 3; 2; 1; 0

Page 24
2 mittens, 1 pair; 2 boots, 1 pair; 4 socks, 2 pairs; 4 shoes, no pairs; 6 gloves, 2 pairs (and 2 odd ones); 5 scarves, no pairs
Extra: 6 pairs altogether

Page 27
There are 24 stars on the tree.

Page 28
36 small triangles; 72 triangles in total (we think!)

Page 30
Sam, 6.00; Izzie, 7.00; Ranjit, 6.30; Carla, 10.30; Joe, 8.00; Kylie, 10.00. Extra: Sam; Carla

Page 31
tallest: Ranjit's; fattest: Sam's; shortest: Joe's; thinnest: Carla's; Joe's and Kylie's; 5

Page 34
Extra: 1000

Page 37
cone; cuboid; tetrahedron; pyramid; cylinder; sphere
Extra: rectangle and 2 circles

Page 41
bauble: down, 60p; cracker: up, 30p; pudding: up, £1.30; Santa: down, 40p; popper: down, 10p; card: up, 40p; mince pie: down, 50p; paper chain: up, £1.00
Extra: either is right

Page 42
12, 13, 20; 15, 30, 4; 32, 20, 50; 9, 100, 44; 28, 18, 54

Page 48
5, 10, 15, 20, 25, 30, 35, 40, 45, 50, 55, 60, 65, 70, 75, 80, 85, 90, 95, 100; 20 surprises; 10, 20, 30, 40, 50, 60, 70, 80, 90, 100; 10 spiders
Extra: 10

Published by Brilliant Publications
Sales and despatch:
BEBC Brilliant Publications
Albion Close, Parkstone, Poole, Dorset, BH12 3LL
Tel: 01202 712910
Fax: 0845 1309300
email: brilliant@bebc.co.uk
website:www.brilliantpublications.co.uk

Editorial and marketing:
Brilliant Publications
Unit 10, Sparrow Hall Farm, Edlesborough, Dunstable
Bedfordshire LU6 2ES

The name Brilliant Publications and the logo are registered trademarks.

ISBN-13...978-1-903853-68-9

Written by Irene Yates
Illustrated by Gaynor Berry
Cover design by Z2 Graphics
Cover illustration by Chantal Kees

First published in 2005, reprinted 2008.
10 9 8 7 6 5 4 3 2

Printed in the UK
© Irene Yates 2005

Contents

Introduction

This book has been designed to take you through the term leading up to Christmas, with the targets of the Key Stage 1 Numeracy Strategy autumn term for Reception and Years 1 and 2 specifically in mind. The book, as a whole, covers a wide spectrum of these targets whilst providing lots of fun activities all linked to Christmas.

The sheets can be used independently and most ask the children to work in the space provided. There are a few activities which require cutting and sticking; these have a scissors symbol in the corner (✂). Each task, or activity, has educational rigour, making the work suitable for introducing a topic or reinforcing it. The sheets are not designed as time fillers and should not be used as such. They are meant to become an integral part of your Numeracy planning for the first term of the year.

The elves' speech bubbles on every sheet are useful starting points for plenary sessions.

The contents page provides brief descriptions of the Numeracy objectives for each sheet. Using these brief descriptions you can run down the contents page to find objectives you want to reinforce with particular children. You can tick them off to remind yourself of the targets you have worked on.

Where sheets have specific answers, these are given on page 2.

This book is one of a series of books aimed at making your life easier around Christmas time. The other books in the series are:

Christmas Activities for KS1 Language and Literacy   ISBN-10...1-905853-66-4
                                                       ISBN-13...978-903853-66-5
Christmas Activities for KS2 Language and Literacy   ISBN-10...1-903853-67-2
                                                       ISBN-13...978-1-903853-67-2
Christmas Activities for KS2 Maths   ISBN-10...1-903853-69-9
                                                       ISBN-13...978-1-903853-69-6

Have fun!

Make Christmas spirals

Does everyone's spiral turn round the same way?

Colour in your spiral.
Cut along the line.
Thread some cotton through the dot.
Hang the spirals up.

Christmas stocking

Cut out all the presents.
How many can you fit into
the stocking without going
over the edges?
Stick on the ones that fit.

Are any
presents left
over?

Christmas teddies

Cut out the teddies.
Cut out the chimney pots.
Stick each teddy to the chimney that it just fits.

Draw a teddy of your own. Make a chimney for it to fit into.

Christmas Activities for KS1 Maths

Stars 1

Which star is the odd one out?

Draw a picture of the one that is different.

In what ways is the star different?

Stars 2

Draw lines to join the stars that match.

Draw a star of your own that has nothing the same as any of these stars.

Christmas tree

Here is half of a
Christmas tree.
Draw the other half.

How many baubles
are on the whole tree?

Christmas count

How many Christmas trees?

How many stars?

How many Santas?

How many presents?

How many things are there altogether on the page?

Another Christmas count

Count the mince pies.

Count the Christmas puddings.

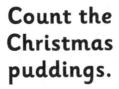

Count the candles.

When you have counted <u>down</u> the columns, count <u>up</u> the columns.

Are the answers the same?

Count the presents

Santa needs lots of presents to give to the children,
but does he know how many he has?

Count the teddies. ☐

Count the cars. ☐

Count the trains. ☐

Count the elephants. ☐

How many
are in the
biggest
group? ☐

Count the toys. ☐

Christmas Activities for KS1 Maths

How many chimneys?

Santa has all these sacks of toys.

Draw one chimney for each sack of toys.

How many chimneys did you draw?

Nearly ready!

Santa is nearly ready. Have a look at the sleigh.

How many
sacks?

How many
sacks?

How many
sacks?

How many
sacks?

How many
sacks?

Is there room
for one more?

Christmas Activities for KS1 Maths

Nearly finished

Santa is nearly finished. Have a look at the sleigh.

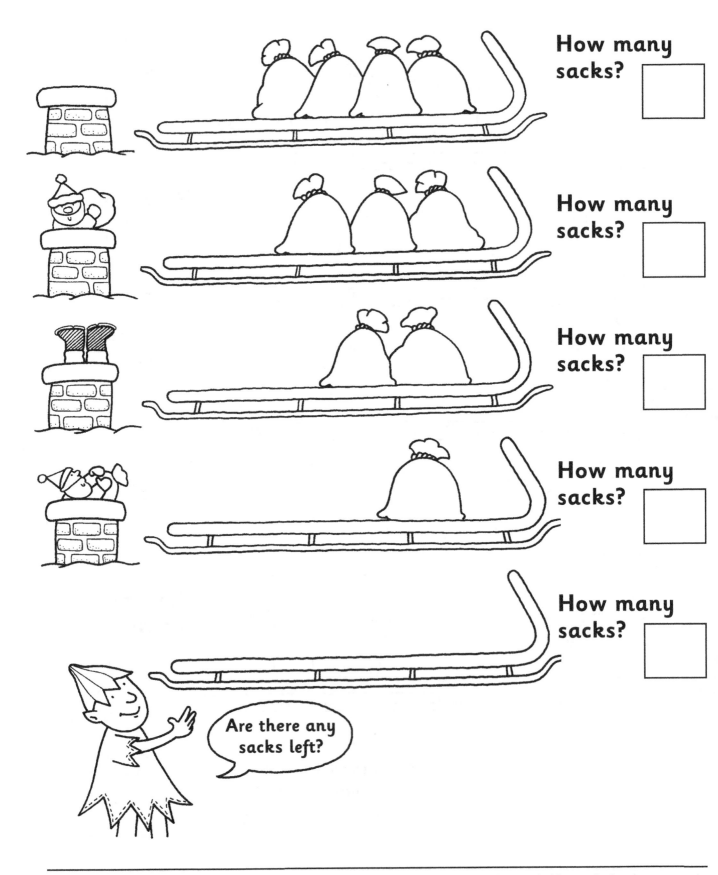

How many sacks? ☐

How many sacks? ☐

How many sacks? ☐

How many sacks? ☐

How many sacks? ☐

Are there any sacks left?

Santa's muddle

Look at the houses. The numbers are on the doors.

Look at the sleigh. The sacks are all in the wrong order. The children will get the wrong presents.

Draw a sleigh and put the sacks in the right order.

How many houses are there? ☐

How many sacks are there? ☐

Sharing out

Santa has a lot of teddies. He needs to share them out.
Can you help him?

Cut out all the teddies.
Put the teddies into two groups.

How many teddies are in each group?

Santa's problem

The house numbers have fallen off the houses!
Santa needs to put them back so he can deliver the presents.

One side of the street has even numbers, starting at 16.
The other side has odd numbers, starting at 15.

Put the numbers on the houses.

Remember to count in twos.

Christmas decorations

Sam has made some decorations.
He has made 3 triangles △ △ △
                     3 circles ○○○
and   3 squares. □□□

He wants to hang them up in repeating patterns.
How many different patterns can he make?

Draw them here:

Try adding another shape.
How many patterns can
you make now?

Santa's dozen

Santa has 12 presents. How many children should he give them to? How many presents should they have each?

Write as many ways as you can of making 12.

What is the highest number of children who could have a present? ☐

How many would they have each? ☐

Twenty things for Santa

Think of **20** different things to do with Christmas.
Draw them or write about them in the Christmas tree.

Count again to make sure you have 20 things.

Snowmen game

Cut out the snowmen. Stick them in a line on another piece of paper, starting with the biggest.

Cut out another page of snowmen and stick them in a line, starting with the smallest.

Christmas Activities for KS1 Maths

Santa's pairs

Santa has a lot of pairs of things to deliver. Make sure he has the pairs right.

How many mittens? ☐
How many pairs? ☐

How many boots? ☐
How many pairs? ☐

How many socks? ☐
How many pairs? ☐

How many shoes? ☐
How many pairs? ☐

How many gloves? ☐
How many pairs? ☐

How many scarves? ☐
How many pairs? ☐

How many pairs altogether? ☐

Christmas toys

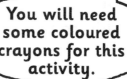

The elves have set the toys out in a row to make the packing easy.

You will need some coloured crayons for this activity.

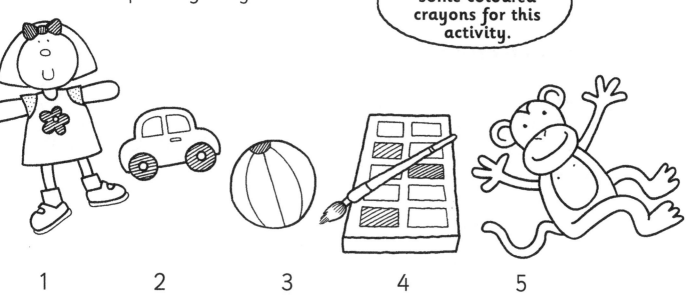

1　　　　2　　　　3　　　　4　　　　5

Colour the first toy green.

Colour the second toy yellow.

Colour the third toy red.

Colour the fourth toy blue.

Colour the fifth toy brown.

Draw the toy that is last in the row in this box.

If I put this toy after the monkey, what number will it be?

Santa's sacks

Santa has ten sacks.
There are ten children hoping to get a present.

Draw lines to match the sacks with the boys and girls.

Guess the stars

Without counting, guess how many stars are on the tree.
Write your guess here. ☐

Now count the stars. How many are there? ☐

Are there <u>fewer</u> stars than your guess? ☐

Are there <u>more</u> stars than your guess? ☐

What is the difference between your guess and the count? ☐

Write this down as a sum:

Add some more stars and ask a friend to guess and count.

Triangle Christmas tree

Look at the Christmas tree.
It is made of triangles.

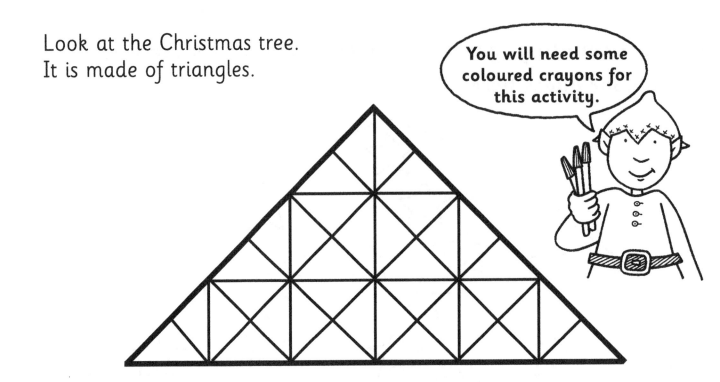

You will need some coloured crayons for this activity.

Guess how many triangles there are.

Count how many triangles there are.

Is your count the same as your guess?

Use four colours to colour the triangles in a pattern.

Can you think of a way of making more triangles by adding just three horizontal lines? Have a go.

Christmas calendar

What day is it today?

What date is it?

How many days until Christmas?

> Decorate your calendar with Christmas pictures and patterns.

Make a calendar from today until Christmas Day.

Cross the days off until Christmas.

Sunday	Monday	Tuesday	Wednesday	Thursday	Friday	Saturday

Bed-time

Santa will bring the presents only when the children are fast asleep.

Write what time the children go to bed.

Sam

Izzie

Ranjit

Carla

Joe

Kylie

Who is the earliest to bed?

Who is the latest to bed?

Snowmen

All the children have made a snowman.

Sam's
snowman

Izzie's
snowman

Ranjit's
snowman

Carla's
snowman

Joe's
snowman

Kylie's
snowman

Whose snowman is the tallest? _____

Whose snowman is the fattest? _____

Whose snowman is the shortest? _____

Whose snowman is the thinnest? _____

Whose snowmen are shorter than Izzie's? _____

How many snowmen are fatter than Carla's?

_____

Christmas presents

Use your fingers to measure across the Christmas presents.

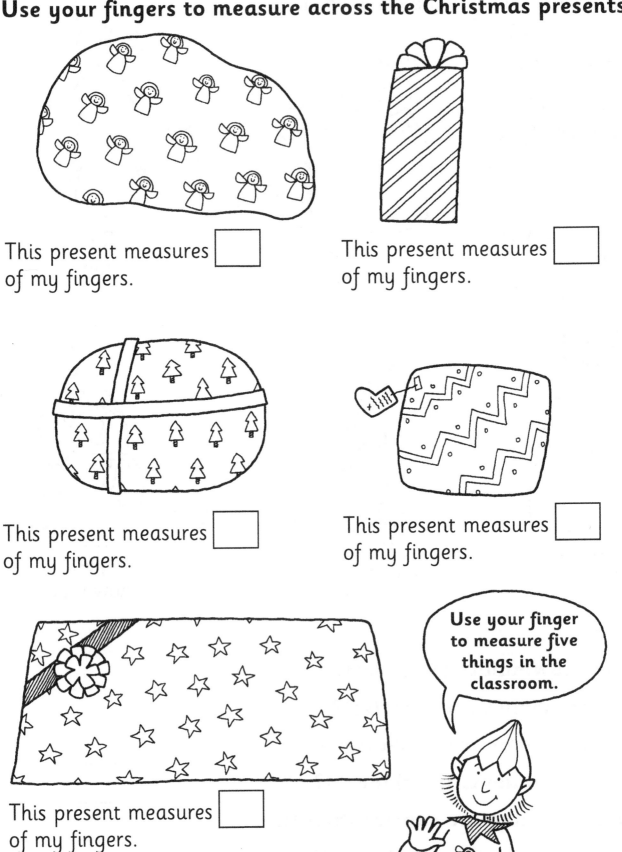

This present measures ☐
of my fingers.

This present measures ☐
of my fingers.

This present measures ☐
of my fingers.

This present measures ☐
of my fingers.

This present measures ☐
of my fingers.

Use your finger
to measure five
things in the
classroom.

Santa's sleigh

Guess how many sacks you think will fit on Santa's sleigh.
Use your finger to help you.

Cut out the sacks. Carefully stick them on the sleigh so they
don't overlap.

How many sacks did you fit on?

Was your guess close?

Santa's big night

Santa has a hundred parcels to deliver in this street. The houses are numbered 1 to 100. **Write the numbers on the houses.**

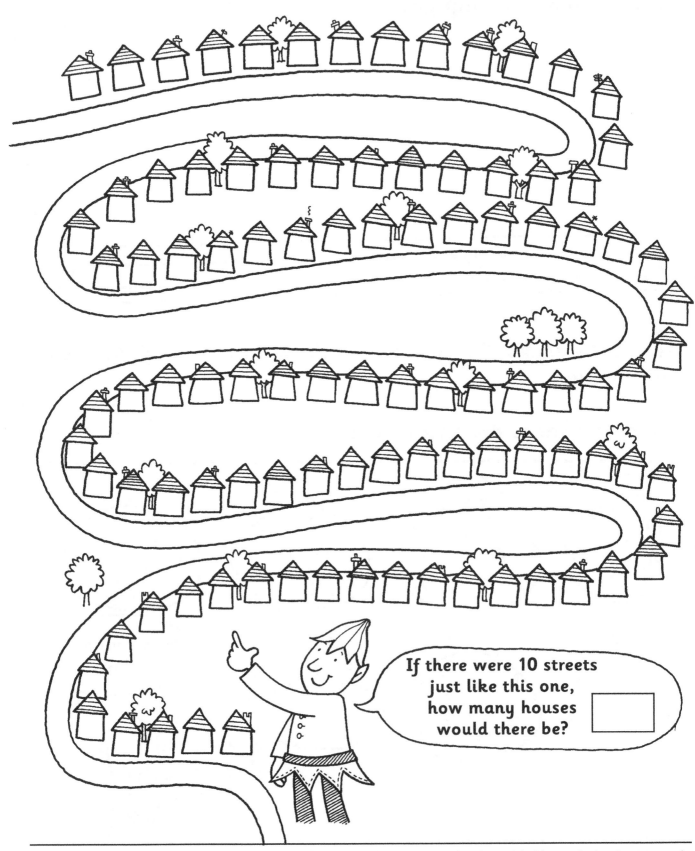

If there were 10 streets just like this one, how many houses would there be?

Buying presents

Joe has £2.00 to spend on presents for his little sister.

Work out four different ways he can spend his £2.00.

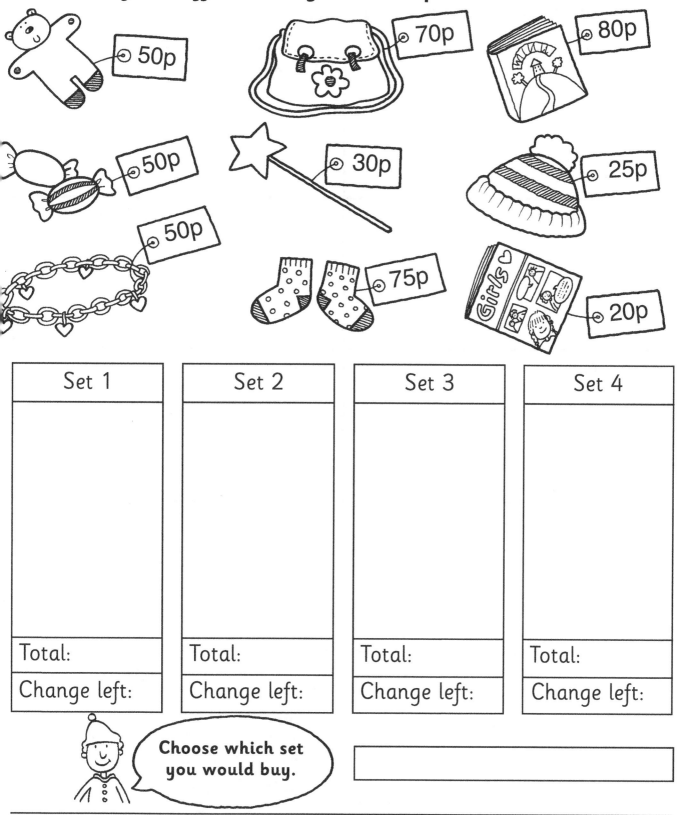

Set 1	Set 2	Set 3	Set 4
Total:	Total:	Total:	Total:
Change left:	Change left:	Change left:	Change left:

Choose which set you would buy.

2-D Christmas tree decorations

Izzie is making decorations for the Christmas tree. She has lots of card and glue and glitter. She is making 2-D (flat) shapes.

Draw the shapes for her to cut out.

A circle	A hexagon
A triangle	A triangle with a right angle
A pentagon	A square
A rectangle	A half circle
An octagon	Make decorations of your own. Thread string through the top to hang them up.

3-D Christmas tree decorations

Joe has made these decorations.

Name the shapes.

Which 2-D shapes is a
cylinder made out of?

Word box

cone   cuboid

cylinder   pyramid

sphere   tetrahedron

Starry night

Fill in the sums for each star.

The first two are done for you.

1
1 + 0 = 1
0 + 1 = 1

2
1 + 1 = 2
2 + 0 = 2
0 + 2 = 2

3

4

5

6

7

8

10

9

Count how many number bonds there are for each star. What do you notice?

Starry numbers

Join the dots, counting back in 10s, starting at 180.

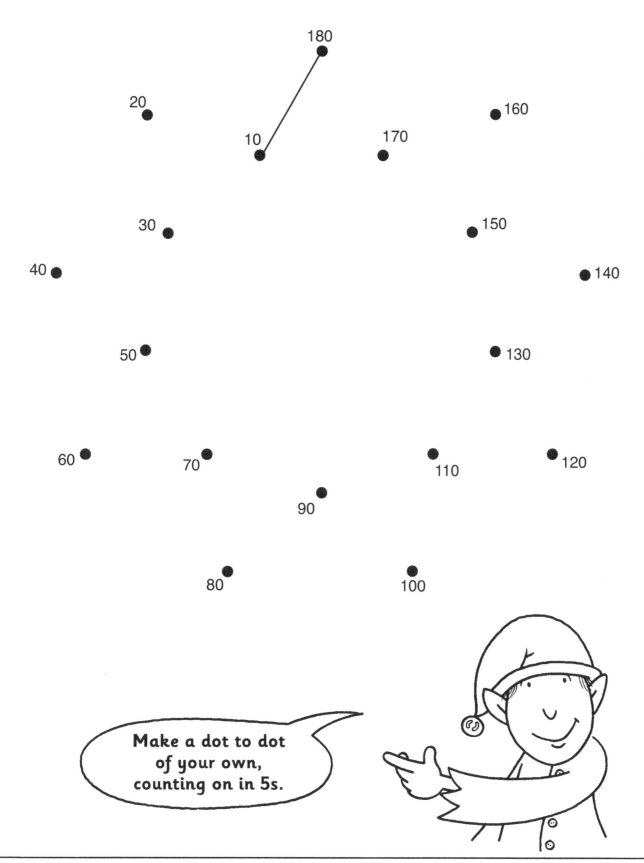

Make a dot to dot
of your own,
counting on in 5s.

Santa's round

In one street Santa has 100 sacks to deliver.
He has:

12 boys' presents   21 toddlers' presents

11 girls' presents   13 dads' presents

15 babies' presents   14 mums' presents

 8 grandmothers' presents   1 dog's present

 5 grandfathers' presents

Which group is the largest?
Which group is the smallest?

Make a block graph to show all these presents.

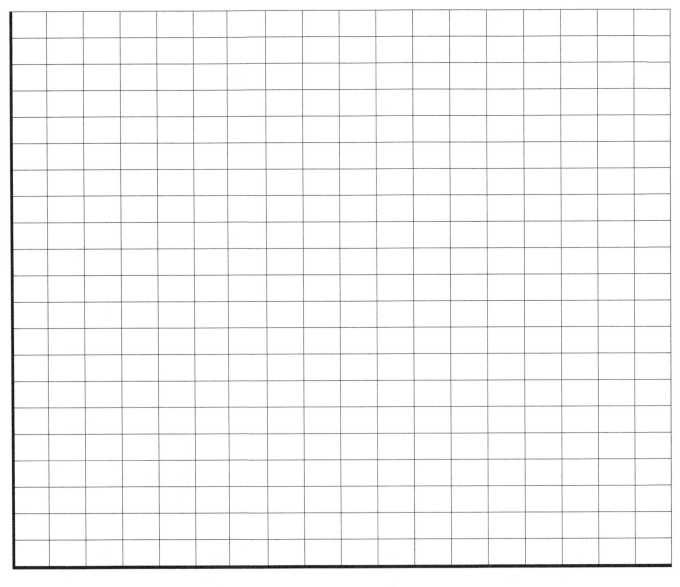

Christmas prices

Look at the prices on these presents. Round each one
to the nearest 10p. Write your rounded price in the star.
In the box show if you have rounded up or down.

	Up / Down
	Up / Down
	Up / Down
	Up / Down
	Up / Down
	Up / Down
	Up / Down
	Up / Down

63p · 27p · £1.29 · 44p · 12p · 38p · 54p · 98p

A candle costs 45p.
Will you round it
up or down?

Christmas crackers

Solve the Christmas crackers.

double
6

half of
26

double
10

half of
30

double
15

half of
8

double
16

half of
40

double
25

half of
18

double
50

half of
88

double
14

half of
36

double
27

If you double your age and then halve it, what do you end with?

Pudding patterns

Cut out the puddings at the bottom of the page.

This is a whole turn.   This is a quarter turn.

This is a half turn.   The is a three-quarter turn.

Use different turns to make four different patterns.

Draw your patterns here:

_____

_____

_____

_____

What happens if you flip the puddings over?

Christmas Activities for KS1 Maths

Christmas cakes

Follow the instructions to colour the Christmas cakes. Write the maths symbol for each section in the box. The first is done for you.

You will need some coloured crayons for this activity.

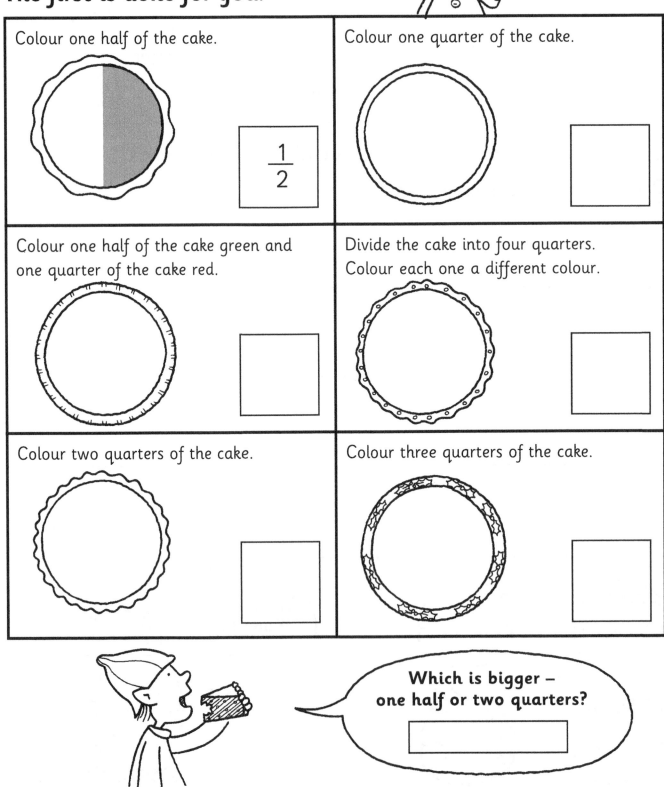

Colour one half of the cake.

$$\frac{1}{2}$$

Colour one quarter of the cake.

Colour one half of the cake green and one quarter of the cake red.

Divide the cake into four quarters. Colour each one a different colour.

Colour two quarters of the cake.

Colour three quarters of the cake.

Which is bigger – one half or two quarters?

Working day

Write the times as on a 24 hour clock as well, if you can.

On Christmas Eve the elves work really hard.
Write the times on the clocks.

The elves start at 5 o'clock in the morning.

They have breakfast at 7 o'clock.

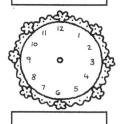

The elves have a break at 10 o'clock.

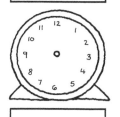

They have lunch at 1 o'clock.

They have tea at 5 o'clock.

They wave Santa off at 8 o'clock.

Christmas times

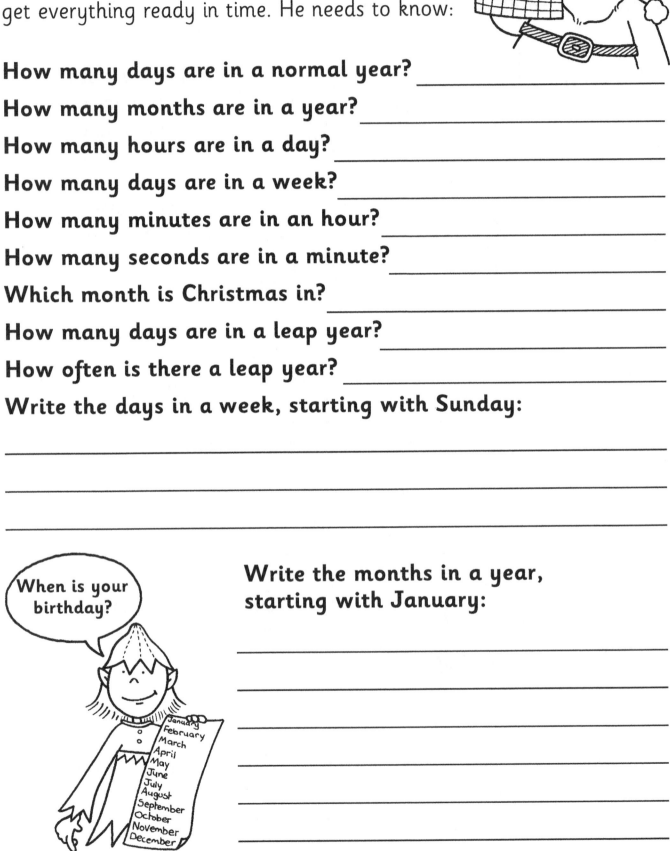

Santa has to work hard all through the year to get everything ready in time. He needs to know:

How many days are in a normal year? _____

How many months are in a year? _____

How many hours are in a day? _____

How many days are in a week? _____

How many minutes are in an hour? _____

How many seconds are in a minute? _____

Which month is Christmas in? _____

How many days are in a leap year? _____

How often is there a leap year? _____

Write the days in a week, starting with Sunday:

_____

_____

_____

When is your birthday?

Write the months in a year, starting with January:

_____

_____

_____

_____

_____

_____

Christmas shapes

What can you draw using some, or all, of these shapes?
You can turn them as much as you like.

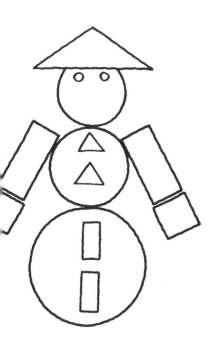

Draw as many pictures as you can. Go on to another page to carry on.

Christmas Activities for KS1 Maths

Surprise, surprise!

Little Elf is filling 100 sacks with presents.
Into every fifth sack, he is putting a surprise.

**Write the numbers of the sacks that
will have the surprises, starting at 5.**

How many sacks will have a surprise in them?

How many
fewer spiders
are there than
surprises?

Mischief Elf is following Little Elf. She is
putting a joke spider in every tenth sack.

**Write the numbers of the sacks that will
have a spider, starting at 10.**

**How many sacks will have
a spider in them?**